SEE INSIDE

AN AIRPORT

Series Editor: **R. J. Unstead**

D0542432

KINGFISHER BOOKS

Series Editor
R. J. Unstead

Author
Jonathan Rutland

Illustrators
John Berry, John Green,
Michael Kelly

Kingfisher Books, Grisewood & Dempsey Ltd,
Elsley House, 24–30 Great Tichfield Street,
London W1P 7AD

This revised edition published in 1988
by Kingfisher Books
Originally published in hardcover in 1977
by Hutchinson & Co (Publishers) Ltd
© Grisewood & Dempsey Ltd 1977, 1988
BRITISH LIBRARY CATALOGUING IN PUBLICATION DATA
Rutland, Jonathan
    See inside an airport.—2nd ed.
    (See inside).
    1. Airports—Juvenile literature
    I. Title
    387.7'36   HE9797
ISBN 0 86272 343 4

Printed in Hong Kong

CONTENTS

*The editors wish to thank Mr Hubert Jessell, formerly Director of
Aerodrome standards with the Civil Aviation Authority, and Mr A. D.
Steed, Assistant Chief Photographic Services, British Airways for
their kind assistance in the preparation of this book.*

Gateway to the Sky

In the early days of air travel there were few passengers and the aircraft were slow and fairly small. Airports were little more than large flat fields, with sheds to shelter waiting passengers and cargo, and hangars for the aeroplanes.

A large modern airport handles between 50 and 100 thousand passengers on a busy day, as well as many hundreds of tonnes of cargo. Aircraft – some of them carrying as many as 400 people – take off and land every few minutes. The airport bustles with activity and people – rather like a small town, complete with shops and offices, buses, taxis and even its own hospital and police force.

To keep everything running smoothly 50,000 or more people work in the airport on jobs ranging from controlling the movements of every aircraft and seeing that passengers are in the right place at the right time, to serving snacks in the restaurants and running the airport shops.

Airports are normally some distance from the city they serve, so that the noise of big jet airliners disturbs as few people as possible. The airport is usually linked to the city centre by motorway and sometimes by railway, but even so passengers flying short distances may take as long travelling out to the airport as they spend in the air. Some cities now have an inner airport for STOL aircraft. STOL stands for Short Take Off and Landing.

Above and below: Aircraft from all over the world fly in and out of international airports night and day. The apron is floodlit at night for loading, unloading and boarding.

Opposite: While waiting for your flight to be called, you can buy refreshments and duty free goods. Each passenger can only take a certain weight of baggage on an aeroplane. Baggage has to be checked by the security officers to prevent smuggling and hi-jacking.

1 Runway	6 Control tower
2 Taxiway	7 Airport roads
3 Apron	8 Cargo terminal
4 Terminal building	9 Fuel store
5 Pier	10 Aircraft hangars

An International Airport

The illustration shows the layout of a typical international airport. The runways (1) are parallel and in line with the prevailing wind – so that planes take off and land into the wind. This increases the speed of the air flowing over the wings, to provide the plane with more lift (see Glossary on page 28). Taxiways (2) link the runways with the apron (3) – near the terminal where aircraft park between flights for loading, unloading and servicing.

Long piers (5) jut out across the apron, linking each plane at its 'stand' to the terminal buildings. The piers provide places for a large number of planes, and they allow passengers to travel to and from their aircraft under cover (often along moving 'walkways'). There is also room on the apron for the many vehicles needed to service and refuel each plane between flights.

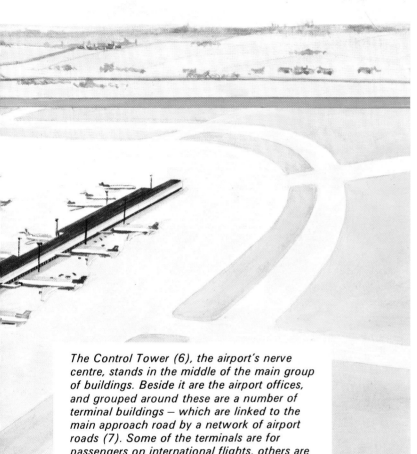

The Control Tower (6), the airport's nerve centre, stands in the middle of the main group of buildings. Beside it are the airport offices, and grouped around these are a number of terminal buildings – which are linked to the main approach road by a network of airport roads (7). Some of the terminals are for passengers on international flights, others are for those on internal flights. There is also a special cargo terminal (8). Aircraft fuel is stored in the installation (9) beyond. There are also huge hangars (10) where the aircraft are serviced.

Below: The airport fire service on a practice exercise. Safety is vitally important at airports. The emergency services – fire and ambulance – are always on the alert and can rush to the scene of an accident in seconds. Chemical foam is used to smother flames and fire fighters wear special protective clothing.

Control Tower

From their look-out point at the top of the control tower, air traffic control and ground control officers watch the movements of all aircraft on the runways and taxiways and around the apron. In a darkened room lower down in the tower, approach control officers direct aircraft coming in to land (see pages 18–19). Helped by computers and other electronic aids, the ground control officers must plan the exact route of each plane as it moves through the airport. Equally important, they must decide precisely when each move should be made, and radio the information to the pilot – and to the drivers of all the fuel, maintenance and other vehicles attending the planes during turn-round. As there may be a great many aircraft in the airport at one time, the work is very complicated. The smallest mistake or misunderstanding could lead to disaster. Imagine, for example, what would happen if a plane taxied out on to a runway along which another plane was taking off.

If anything should go wrong, the officers quickly alert the emergency services (fire, ambulance, for instance) and warn other planes and vehicles nearby. Very occasionally air traffic control has to deal with an emergency landing – a plane's undercarriage (landing wheels) may have jammed. In this event, the controllers clear the runway and alert the emergency services, before allowing the pilot to land.

The air traffic and ground controllers should be able to see the positions and movements of all aircraft at all times. Even when visibility is bad – for example at night, or in fog – their special radar screens (above) give them a clear 'picture' of the runways, taxiways and aprons, and all aircraft in the airport.

Right: To ensure the smooth and safe running of the airport, officers in the control tower are in radio contact with: runway clearance services; the passenger terminals; meteorological offices; security forces; ambulances; the pilot; and the fire service.

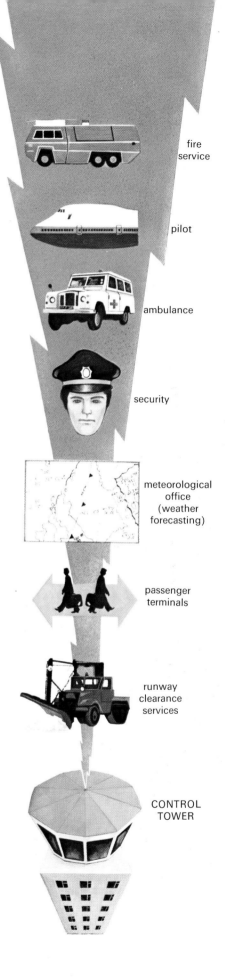

fire service

pilot

ambulance

security

meteorological office (weather forecasting)

passenger terminals

runway clearance services

CONTROL TOWER

The Concourse

Once passengers' luggage has been handed over at the check-in desk, it is weighed, and labelled with a special tag showing flight number and destination. It then disappears along a conveyor (see round panel on left of main picture), and the owner will not see it again until the end of his journey. The conveyor takes it to a central point where all the luggage is sorted into flights. As soon as the luggage for one flight is assembled, it is taken out on a truck and loaded into the aircraft (the lower part of the fuselage, beneath the passenger cabins, is used for luggage and other cargo). When the plane arrives at its destination, the process is reversed. As the passengers disembark, their cases are unloaded and taken to the baggage reclaim hall. There the luggage travels round and round on a circular 'carousel' until taken off by its owners.

Passport

Boarding pass

When you arrive at the airport, your first task is to find the correct terminal building. Once there, you enter the huge departures hall – part of the concourse – where you will see rows of check-in desks (each airline usually has its own). At the desk you hand over your ticket, which is checked by means of a computer (square panel, top left). The computer stores details of every ticket issued, and can show how many seats are booked on each flight. You also hand over your baggage.

In return you will receive a boarding pass, which shows your flight number, your seat number on the plane, and the departure gate you must go through when your flight is called (see pages 14–15). If there is time, you can now visit the shops, banks, snack bars and restaurants around the concourse.

To avoid passenger 'traffic jams', arrivals and departures are on different levels. You can see part of the arrivals hall on the right of the main picture. Passengers collect their luggage, and after passing through passport control and customs (round panel, top right) they can leave. In the arrivals hall of the concourse are notices in several languages telling passengers where they can find buses, taxis, trains, and hotels.

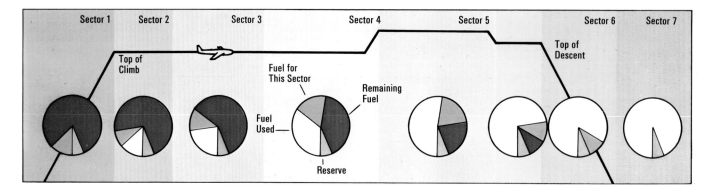

Sector 1   Sector 2   Sector 3   Sector 4   Sector 5   Sector 6   Sector 7

Top of Climb

Fuel for This Sector

Remaining Fuel

Fuel Used

Top of Descent

Reserve

Above: A typical fuel flight plan. The captain divides his route into sectors, and works out how much fuel is needed for each. This depends on the load, the height at which he flies, and the strength and direction of the wind. In this plan the amount of fuel needed for each sector is shown in orange. The mauve segment shows the reserve — extra fuel carried in case of emergency (for example, bad weather may force the plane to land at a more distant airport).

Below: A busy scene in the Operations and Control Room. Here details are worked out to ensure that every flight is safe, smooth and pleasant.

Airline Operations and Control Room

While you wait for your flight to be called, staff are busy on last minute details in the airline's operations and control room. Load control assistants receive details of passenger luggage and other cargo being carried, and of the amount of fuel (see diagram, left). They then calculate the aircraft's take-off weight (which includes the weight of the plane and of everything and everyone on board), and its landing weight (take-off weight less the weight of the fuel used during the flight). Safety regulations give the maximum weights allowed for each type of airliner. Finally the load controllers work out how the cargo should be stowed, and how the fuel should be distributed between the fuel tanks. If the loads are not carefully balanced, the plane may be nose or tail heavy – and difficult to handle.

The captain and his flight crew are also in the operations and control room, working out the flight plan (see right), and the cabin staff arrive to collect the passenger list and to receive any special instructions (perhaps one of the passengers is unwell and needs extra care).

Other members of the airline staff keep track of every airliner in their fleet as they fly around the world. They call up any service vehicles needed during 'turn around' (the period between a plane finishing one flight and taking off on the next) and also see to countless other details.

THE FLIGHT PLAN

The flight plan gives details of the plane, the route, the height and the speed at which the captain intends to fly on each section of the route. It gives the time he expects to arrive at various points, and the ETA (estimated time of arrival). Before completing the flight plan the captain consults the meteorological department – wind strengths affect his speed, and he may need to alter height or course to avoid bad weather or to take advantage of a following wind. Finally, he submits his plan to Air Traffic Control for approval. They check that the route, flight level and time interval keep him well clear of other aircraft, and they pass details on to air traffic controllers along the route and at the destination.

Between Flight Service

Before a plane touches down, all the vehicles and people needed for its between-flight service will have been alerted, so that the moment it parks at its stand work can begin. A mobile generator (1) is linked to the plane to provide electricity. Customs officers come on board to check the stocks of duty-free goods (which can only be sold when the plane is airborne). Gangs of workmen with trucks and trailers (2) and special scissors-lift transporters (3) arrive to unload luggage and other cargo. Other scissors-lift trucks bring cleaners and caterers, and lift them up to the fuselage service doors high off the ground. The cleaners tidy the cabins and empty the lavatories (using a suction pump which takes the waste to a service tanker). The caterers bring on pre-packed food for the next flight, and remove dirty crockery and cutlery. A small tanker arrives with water.

REFUELLING

Before refuelling begins a technician takes a sample of fuel from the plane's tanks to make sure that it is clean (any dirt could clog the pipes taking fuel to the engines). The plane may be refuelled from a huge tanker, or it may be linked by a hose to underground pipes which carry fuel to the apron from the airport's fuel installation. A large jet airliner holds over 100,000 litres of aviation fuel (and when in flight it uses over two litres every second), so even though powerful pumps deliver 4500 litres a minute, refuelling takes some time.

FLIGHT REPORT

After each flight the captain writes his flight report. In it he mentions anything unusual that happened, and asks for checks to be made. Routine checks include everything from the engines and electric and hydraulic control systems to the navigation lights, brakes and tyres. The engineer in charge will not authorize take-off unless he is sure that the plane is in perfect order.

Boarding and Customs

Once they have handed over their luggage and received a boarding pass at the check-in desk, passengers wait in the departure hall for the announcement calling them to their flight. Passengers on internal flights have only to show their tickets or boarding passes at the barrier before boarding their aircraft. International passengers show their passports and go through a security check into a departure lounge. The security officers use electronic scanners to detect any metal objects (such as guns) hidden in clothing or luggage.

The moment passengers pass into the departure lounge, they are, in effect, abroad. In the departure lounge are shops where duty-free goods can be bought. At last a loudspeaker announcement calls passengers to their gate, where a member of the airline staff waits to lead them to their aircraft. In the picture you can see enclosed 'walkways' or 'air jetties' that lead to the planes. The walkways are hinged where they join the main building, supported on wheels at the other end, and their length can be altered by telescoping them. At some airports airliners park well away from the terminal building, and travellers are driven out to their planes by bus.

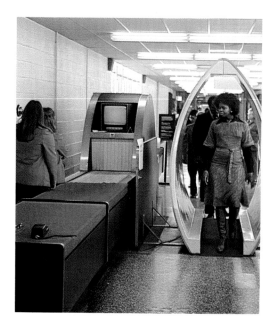

Passengers on international flights are checked by security officers before boarding the aircraft. Electronic scanners are used to check the passengers themselves, as well as their hand luggage, for hidden weapons.

ANYTHING TO DECLARE?

Many of the staff in the airport work for the airport itself. Many others work for the airlines. Others are government employees, including the customs, immigration and health control officers. Anyone arriving from a country where certain dangerous infectious diseases exist will be checked by health control officials. If a passenger from abroad has no vaccination certificate he may be refused entry. All travellers from abroad have their passports checked by an immigration officer. Finally travellers from abroad must pass through customs. The customs officers see that no one smuggles in goods on which they should pay an import duty (such as watches or cameras), or forbidden goods – such as drugs, or animals.

Passengers are welcomed aboard by the cabin staff. After take-off meals are served. But the cabin staff are not just flying waiters. They are highly trained – to reassure the nervous, to deal with any emergency, to give first aid, and generally to make sure everyone enjoys a safe, comfortable flight.

Ground Control and Take-Off

As soon as everyone is on board, the doors firmly closed and the air jetty away, the captain and his crew begin a series of routine pre-flight checks on their aircraft. At the same time an official on the apron makes sure that all service vehicles are out of the way – all, that is, except for the mobile generator which will supply power to start the engines, and the tractor which will tow the aircraft away from its stand.

The captain now radios the ground controller in the control tower for permission to start the engines. Once this is done the generator drives off, the crew perform further checks (on the engines), and the captain asks Ground Control for clearance to move across the apron to the taxiway. He will be told which

taxiways to follow, and which runway to use. After taxi-ing to the end of the runway, the crew wait until Air Traffic Control gives final permission for take-off. Then, with the brakes on, the captain opens up the engines, makes further pre-flight checks, releases the brakes – and at last the aircraft is speeding along the runway for take-off.

Normally everything goes smoothly. The plane accelerates down the runway and takes off. But should anything go wrong the captain must know at once whether there is enough room ahead for him to stop safely. Marks along the runway give him this infor-

Left: The flight deck of a jet liner. The captain sits on the left with his co-pilot on the right. At take-off they share the work, one steering and the other watching the instruments. Both pilots have a control column (the U shaped 'stick' in front) which operates the elevators and ailerons (hinged flaps on tail and wings), and a rudder bar. The throttles controlling the engines are between the pilots. The mass of instruments on the flight deck show the pilots whether or not they are flying straight and level; they show the flight engineer whether the engines are working correctly, and they show the plane's course and position, and how much fuel is left.

ON THE RUNWAY

The airport has a team of maintenance engineers to keep the runway in good condition, and to vacuum it clean (stones or any other objects could puncture a tyre or make a plane jolt or swerve dangerously).

Birds may also cause trouble. They can break the windscreen, and may even be sucked into the engines. Some airports have a special 'scarecrow' truck with a siren to frighten birds away (above).

mation. Every plane carries a chart that shows which runway mark is the point of no return for that particular plane. There is generally a stretch of clear ground ahead of the runway in case of any disaster at take-off or landing. For large jets the runway itself needs to be about $3\frac{1}{2}$ km long, and is made of concrete over half a metre thick. The surface is often ribbed – this gives the wheels a good grip, and helps rainwater to flow away quickly.

Usually the plane climbs to a safe height of about 450 m. The captain then cuts back the engines to reduce noise until he is well clear of the city.

Right: The Air Traffic Control room at night. The picture also shows the runway lights which guide pilots during night operations. White lights mark the edges of the runways. Green lights show the near end ('near' for an aircraft coming in to land), and red ones the far end. In addition there are usually lights down the centre of the runway, and others showing the actual touch-down area. Before the start of the runway, a row of lights help pilots line up for their final approach.

Approach Control

As his airliner takes off, the pilot confirms the first leg of his route with Air Traffic Control. But within a few minutes he passes out of the airport's control and is directed on to and along his route by other air traffic control centres – and by radio transmitters which provide invisible pathways through the sky to guide him.

Then, as he approaches the end of his journey he contacts Approach Control in the control tower at his destination airport. Often there is a queue of aircraft waiting to land and Approach Control will direct him to a 'stack' – a group of planes circling one above the other, each safely separated from its neighbours by about 300 m in height. The plane at the bottom of the stack is normally first in the queue, and when it leaves the others all move down a 'step'. There may be several stacks, and procedural control officers in Approach Control decide which should have the next turn.

As each aircraft leaves the stack it becomes the responsibility of a radar controller (large picture). He can see the plane's exact position and altitude on his radar screen, and his job is to guide the pilot towards the airport – and to see that all the planes coming in under his control are correctly separated. Having them too far apart wastes time, while allowing them too close together could lead to a collision. Normally two planes coming in to land on the same runway will be kept at least $6\frac{1}{2}$ km (some 90 seconds in time) apart.

As the plane flies nearer, it is passed on to another radar controller, who guides it into position for the final approach. Sometimes this controller continues to direct the pilot until touch-down ('talking down' is almost invariably used in fog). But usually the controller guides the pilot into position for the final approach, and then directs him to use the Instrument Landing System (ILS – see diagrams). As soon as the pilot is on the ILS beam, he switches his radio to a new frequency to receive final instructions and clearance to land from Air Traffic Control.

Below: The Instrument Landing System (ILS). After circling in the stack (which is marked by a radio beacon), the plane gets into position for its final approach, locking into ILS radio beams. One, the localizer, ensures that the plane is exactly in line with the runway. Another, the glide path, marks the correct angle of descent. An instrument (below left) shows whether the plane is properly lined-up (as in the middle example). If the vertical needle points to the right, the pilot must fly right to get on the localizer beam. If the horizontal needle points down (top) he must fly down to get into the glide path beam. The vertical marker beams tell the pilot his distance from the runway.

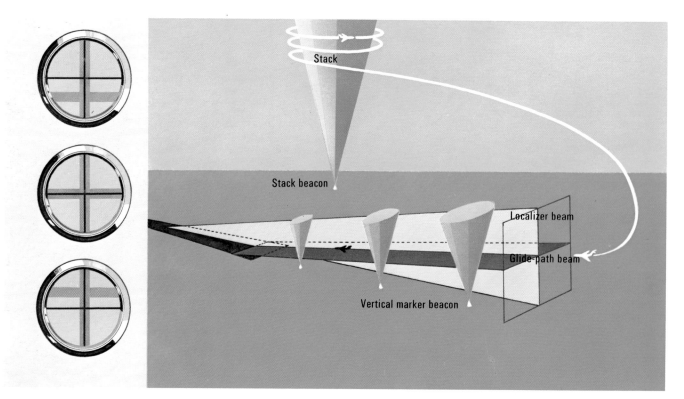

Stack

Stack beacon

Localizer beam

Glide-path beam

Vertical marker beacon

TWA 677

PAN-A 771

TWA 677

TAS 776

FIN 707/1

TWA 747

CIL No29 APR 21
220/09 KT
500/m DRIZZLE
600/0LI
600   69/09
BM17

*Left: A radar controller
in the Approach Control
Room.*

The Freight Terminal

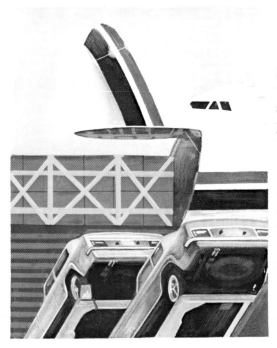

On some freight aircraft the entire nose (as above) or tail can be swung up, or to one side, to speed loading and to make it easier to handle extra large items.

Sending freight by air is expensive, but it is quick and safe, and the airport's freight terminal is always busy. There are consignments of urgent medical supplies, fragile electronic goods, perishable foods and flowers, newspapers, and mail – and much else.

Goods arriving at the terminal are checked in and labelled. Small and medium-sized packages are placed on automatic conveyors, while larger ones may be handled by forklift trucks or robot cranes. Details of each package (its weight, contents, value, airline and destination) are fed into a computer. This calculates the amount of duty due and works out the 'cargo manifest' – a detailed list of the freight carried on each flight.

As the packages travel along the conveyors electronic eyes read their computer-typed labels and operate automatic mechanisms which see that each item is routed to the right aircraft. When goods reach the end of a conveyor, most are packed in special wire-mesh 'boxes' designed to fit snugly into the aircraft's curved hold. Some freight arrives at the terminal ready-packed in large standard-sized containers which are not opened until they reach their destination.

Right: Many millions of animals travel by air each year. Most are transported in special crates or slings to protect them, and are well cared for by expert staff. This baby elephant is enjoying its bottle at the animal hostel while waiting for its plane. Tropical and arctic rooms and pools are provided at the best airports for the comfort of travelling animals, and there is a good stock of all sorts of foodstuffs.

Below: A jumbo jet freighter being loaded. Small items are brought out on trailers and loaded up the sloping conveyor (which can be adjusted to different heights). Containers and wire-mesh 'boxes' are raised up and rolled into the hold on special lift platforms. Customs officers patrol the area at all times, on the alert for smugglers.

The Service Dock

Just as the family car must be serviced at regular intervals, so must an airliner – but the tests and checks are far more thorough. A major check takes place about every three years. This represents some 12,000 flying hours for planes on long distance flights, or 6,000 for short haul aircraft. The greatest stresses on a plane come at landing and take-off, which explains why short haul airliners need servicing after much fewer flying hours than their long haul brothers.

A major check takes nearly two weeks. The plane is stripped down, and each part is tested and examined. Damaged or faulty components must be repaired or replaced, and certain items are replaced at regular intervals even if they show no signs of wear.

The engineer in charge of operations has a large progress

Above: Complex electrical equipment is removed from the plane and checked in the service dock's laboratory.

Left: During a small-scale service, and for routine between-flight checks, the engineer can be raised up by a special vehicle called a 'cherry-picker'. From his vantage point he can check the navigation lights, for example, or examine and make adjustments to the elevator mechanisms.

chart listing every check that must be made. As each operation is completed it is ticked on the chart so that supervisors can see that everything is done, and whether progress is on schedule.

Engineers go over the entire airframe with X-ray or ultrasonic equipment, checking the metal for invisible cracks or other faults. Delicate electronic instruments and equipment are removed and taken to dust-free workshops for inspection. The engines are taken out, and after being stripped down and reassembled are run on special test beds in a sound-proofed room. After they have been refitted in the aircraft, they may be given another test. The plane is towed outside, and huge mufflers are fitted to damp down the tremendous noise.

Every minute that an airliner is out of operation in the maintenance shed costs the airline money. So work continues day and night. For its major check the plane must of course be taken out of operation. But when it only needs a small repair or alteration, the work is usually done at night.

All aircraft, and particularly older turboprop types like the one shown here, receive regular servicing. Teams of engineers carry out the routine overhaul, checking every part of the aircraft's fuselage, engines and internal systems. The huge maintenance sheds in which these overhauls are done can take two jumbo jets and are as large as a football field.

Airport Records

Left: Dallas-Fort Worth, Texas is the third busiest airport in the United States, and when complete will have nine runways and 13 terminals. It has a rapid transit shuttle system to carry passengers between the aircraft and the terminal buildings.

Below: London Heathrow is the busiest international airport in the world. Each year some 30 million passengers use the airport, 23 million of them being international travellers. London has two main airports, Heathrow and Gatwick.

Right: The largest airliner is the Boeing 747, which has a maximum take-off weight of 377,840 kg (833,000 lbs). It has a wing span of 59.64 m (195 ft 8 in) and is 70.66 m (231 ft 10 in) long from nose to tail.

Below: A Dash-7 STOL airliner flies over London's City Airport. STOL (Short Take-Off and Landing) aircraft can take off and land on short runways.

IMPORTANT HAPPENINGS

1903

1903 The Wright brothers make the first true powered aeroplane flight at Kitty Hawk in the USA.

1909 Bleriot makes the first flight across open sea – the English Channel. It takes him just over 36 minutes.

1911 Calbraith Rodgers makes the first coast-to-coast flight across the USA. The flight took 49 days and a series of 69 'hops'. The plane crashed 19 times.

1914 The world's first scheduled passenger aeroplane service opens in Florida, USA. The aircraft were flying boats (planes that could land on water).

1918 The first leg of an airmail service across the USA opens, between Washington and New York.

1919 Alcock and Brown make the first non-stop flight across the Atlantic. In the same year scheduled passenger and cargo flights begin from London's Hounslow Airport. The name Hounslow was marked on the grass airstrip so that pilots could identify it more easily from the air.

1919 The French Farman Goliath plane flies the first air service between two countries – France and Belgium.

1919 Nineteen European nations agree on flying laws: the General Rules for Air Traffic Control.

1919 Royal Dutch Airlines (KLM) begins operations; today it is the world's oldest operating airline.

1920s

1924 Two American aircraft make the first flight around the world – the journey took nearly six months.

1925 A famous US airline is founded: Trans World Airways (TWA). Another, Pan American Airways (Pan Am) was founded two years later in 1927.

1928 Charles Kingsford-Smith makes the first flight across the Pacific from the USA to Australia. The journey was made in three stages, one of which was a 4800-km flight across open ocean.

1929 The first passenger service is opened between Britain and India. The 7240-km journey took eight days, and included stretches by train and flying boat. Many of the 'airports' on the route consisted of little more than a shed, and a flat landing strip of stony desert. One, in the Syrian desert, was built like a fort, complete with battlements and watchtowers – to protect passengers from bandits.

1929 Charles Lindbergh makes the first non-stop solo flight across the Atlantic from the USA to France in the monoplane Spirit of St Louis. The flight lasts 33 hours 39 minutes altogether.

1929 The German Dornier Do X flying boat is able to carry 150 passengers. This huge aircraft has 10 engines.

Below: A biplane made by the Wright brothers, Wilbur and Orville making one the earliest powered flights at Kitty Hawk, North Carolina. The Wrights were originally bicycle makers.

1930s

1931 Handley Page HP 42 biplane airliner begins services with Britain's Imperial Airways. It carries up to 38 passengers in great comfort.
1932 After the building of a chain of airports across Africa, the first regular service from London to Cape Town, South Africa, begins.
1933 Wiley Post in a Lockheed Vega flies solo around the world in 115 hours 35 minutes of actual flying time. In all the journey lasted 8 days and was made in a series of 10 separate 'hops'.
1933 The US Boeing 247 is the first all-metal airliner.
1936 First appearance of the Douglas DC-3 airliner, probably the most famous civil aircraft of all time. Over 10,000 were built and in the 1980s more than 500 DC-3s are still flying.
1939 Pan American Airways inaugurate regular service between the USA and Europe.
1952 De Havilland Comet airliners fly the first jet passenger services.
1958 The Boeing 707 jetliner enters service. It becomes the most successful of the first generation of jet airliners.

1959 French Caravelle is the first rear-engined airliner. Putting the engines at the rear reduces the noise in the passenger cabin.
1970 Boeing 747 jumbo jet enters service with Pan Am. It weighed twice as much as any previous airliner and could carry almost 500 passengers.
1974 A record 674 people cram on board an Australian 747 evacuating people trying to escape from a hurricane disaster in Darwin, Australia.
1976 The Anglo-French Concorde starts up supersonic airliner services for passengers to North America.

1980s

1981–2 First flights of new generation of medium-range airliners, Airbus A310, Boeing 757 and 767, that are more fuel efficient and less noisy than previous aircraft.
1987 The London City Airport opens in the heart of London's Dockland area. Special quiet passenger planes, that can use shorter runways for take-off and landing make it possible for airports of the future to be built in cities.

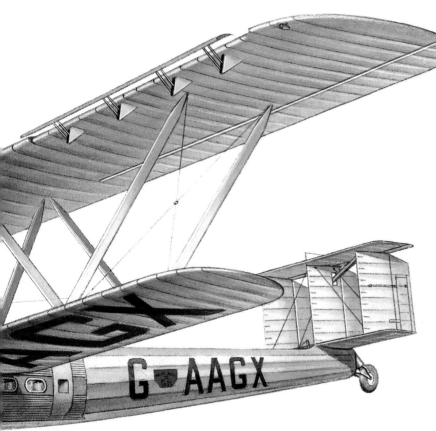

Above: A Handley Page HP 42. This was one of the earliest purpose built airliners, and was used in 1931 by Imperial Airways for its flights in Europe and Africa.

Below: In 1935, the departure hall of London's Croydon airport was described in a picture magazine as 'magnificent'!

GLOSSARY OF TERMS

Aerodrome Old word not often used nowadays for an airfield or airport.

Ailerons Flaps on the trailing edge (back) of the wing of an aeroplane. When extended, they increase the wing area and so increase the amount of lift. Movement of the ailerons controls the plane's attitude.

Air brakes Flaps on the wings or fuselage that are extended to increase drag and so slow down the plane when coming in to land.

Air traffic controller Person who controls movement of aircraft in the air using radar and radio.

Altimeter Instrument that tells a pilot how high the plane is flying above sea level.

Approach lights Lights that guide a pilot towards a runway.

Apron Concrete area near airport buildings for loading and unloading aircraft.

Autopilot Automatic pilot, computerized system that takes over and flies an airliner during long flights.

Control tower Nerve centre of operations at airport, from which incoming and outgoing planes are directed.

Controlled air space Area of sky close to an airport in which airliners waiting to land are controlled, often flying in oval patterns in 'stacks' at different heights.

Drag The air's resistance to an aircraft moving through it.

Elevator Hinged horizontal control surface on the tailplane of an aeroplane, which when moved makes the machine climb or dive.

Flap Moveable part of an aircraft's wing, which when extended increases lift or drag. Used on take-off and landing.

Flight deck Area where pilots sit, formerly known as the cockpit.

Flight plan Plan showing details of an airliner's flight (including destination, route, altitude, speed and fuel carried).

Flight recorder Also known as 'black box', instrument that automatically records details of a flight and often provides useful information in the event of a crash.

Glide path Line of an airliner approaching the runway of an airport.

Ground-controlled approach Radar system for guiding an aircraft in to land.

Hijacking Seizure of an airliner in flight by terrorists.

Holding pattern Course flown by an airliner waiting to land at a busy airport.

ICAO Initials standing for the International Civil Aviation Organization, the world-governing body for civil aviation. Its headquarters are in Montreal, Canada.

Instrument landing system (ILS) System of landing an aircraft automatically, using radio, radar and light signals.

Leading edge Front edge of an aeroplane's wing.

Lift Upward movement of an aeroplane, produced by flow of air over the wings.

Early airports, or aerodromes as they were called at the time, were often rather rough and ready – sometimes just a field and a few huts. The picture below shows Croydon aerodrome, in the outskirts of London, in 1935. It was thought to be very modern and sophisticated in those days.

Mach number Supersonic speeds are measured by Mach numbers, named after the Austrian scientist Ernst Mach (1838–1916). At sea level the speed of sound, at Mach 1, is 1220 km/h (760 mph). At 10,660 m (35,000 ft) where air is colder and thinner, Mach 1 is only 1062 km/h (660 mph).

Navigation lights Lights shown by an airliner at night. Red (port), green (starboard) and white (tail, above and below fuselage) lights flash when the aircraft is flying in a busy area.

Pitch Up and down movement of an aircraft.

Roll Tilting of an aircraft from side to side, controlled by flaps on wings.

Sonic boom Noise made by an aircraft travelling at supersonic speed (above Mach 1) and caused by shock waves.

AIRSPEAK

The International Civil Aviation Organization phonetic alphabet is used worldwide by pilots. English is the international language of flying. Important messages between the pilot and the air traffic controllers could be distorted over the radio. But by using the code words given here, everyone can be sure that their's is received and understood.

A	Alfa	N	November
B	Bravo	O	Oscar
C	Charlie	P	Papa
D	Delta	Q	Quebec
E	Echo	R	Romeo
F	Foxtrot	S	Sierra
G	Golf	T	Tango
H	Hotel	U	Uniform
I	India	V	Victor
J	Juliet	W	Whisky
K	Kilo	X	X-ray
L	Lima	Y	Yankee
M	Mike	Z	Zulu

The unmistakable outline of Concorde, the most advanced passenger airliner in the world. Developed by France and Britain jointly, it can fly at twice the speed of sound (Mach 2), and has halved the time taken to fly across the Atlantic.

Spoilers Control surface on wings that disturb the flow of air over the wings and so increase drag. This slows the aircraft when landing.

STOL Stands for Short Take-Off and Landing.

Thrust Force produced by engines that pushes an aircraft forwards.

Thrust reversers Part of a jet engine that on landing causes the exhaust gases to be deflected forward. This provides 'reverse thrust' to slow down the aircraft.

Trailing edge Rear edge of the wing.

Trim The stable condition of an aircraft in flight.

Above: The Rolls Royce RB-211 turbofan engine.

Below: Turn around – an airliner being prepared for its next journey.

Turbofan Jet engines in which air is sucked in to bypass the engine core and come out as a cold air-stream (rather than as heated gas). This helps to cool the engine, increases efficiency and makes the engine less noisy.

Turn around As soon as an airliner lands, it is checked, cleaned and refuelled ready for its next flight. This is 'turn around'.

Undercarriage Landing gear, or wheels, of an aircraft, folded up into the fuselage and wings after take-off, and let down again just before landing.

Yaw Sideways swivelling movement of an aircraft, controlled by the rudder on the tailplane (fin).

INDEX

PHOTOGRAPHIC ACKNOWLEDGEMENTS
The publishers wish to thank the following for kindly supplying photographs for this book: Page 2 Heathrow Airport Ltd; 3 British Airports; 5 British Airports; 14 Photri; 21 Aeropix Press; 22 P & P F James (Photography) Ltd; 24 *top* Photri, *bottom* P & P F James (Photography) Ltd; 25 *top* Robert Harding, *botton* Mowlem;